Still Human

EMMA STEFANIA

DEDICATION

To all who have come before
and paved the way for the world
to be more enlightened and loving.

CONTENTS

I A Disillusioning Affair   **11**

Karmic Connection   12

Broken   13

A Ghost of the Past   14

Release Is the Path to Peace   15

Breaking Cycles   16

Mending Love   17

Red String of Fate   18

Heartbreak Endures   19

Abandoned Potential   20

Love Fades, Yet Its Memory Lingers   21

Human Love   22

II The Dark Pit of Self   **25**

A Sensitive Soul Grows Weary   26

Spiritual Warfare   27

Self-Protection 28

A Longing for Depth 29

Hazy Thoughts 30

The Sea Speaks 31

Phoenix 32

Break Free 33

Running With the Wolves 34

Interconnected 35

An Old Friend 36

Paradox 37

Strength in Sensitivity 38

III From the Ashes 41

A New Dawn 42

Calm After the Storm 43

Beyond the Surface 44

Divine Love 45

Consciousness Unity 46

Recalibration 47

Creative Sovereignty 48

Beyond the Veil 49

The Promised Land 50

Love Transforms 51

Master or Be Mastered 52

Stand Alone 53

A Tower Moment 54

Love Is a State of Being   55
Beyond the Tears, A Rainbow Awaits   56
Look No Further Than Yourself   57
Cosmic DNA   58
Creation Is One   59
Embrace the Paradox   60
Those in the Shadows   61
Awakening   62
Returning Home   63
Wisdom Awaits on the Other Side   65
Still Human   66

ABOUT THE AUTHOR   69

A Disillusioning Affair

Karmic Connection

Give me a good reason to stay.
You'll find there's no reason to wait until things get better.

They'll never be that way.

You and I were never meant to be.
I should've known that from the start.

You and I are worlds apart.

Broken

Was I wrong for giving you my all?
No.
I was wrong for not leaving anything for *myself.*

Now, here I sit
among the rubble of my heart,
in utter melancholy,
frightened by what I've become.

A Ghost of the Past

Don't call me baby if you can't be there for me.

You ghosted me, and now you're a ghost to me.
A stranger of the past, you never put me first,
only last.

Your words seemed sweet, but they were far from the truth.
And when the truth came out,
I saw a different version of you.

I just didn't want to see.
I gave time for you to grow—to see what you could be.

I was foolish and naïve to believe
that you could change and be there for me.

I can't hold it against you.
It was my mistake, too.

You weren't all to blame;
in many ways, we were the same.

But, at the same time, you wasted my time
for making me believe you'll always be mine.

Release Is the Path to Peace

Your poison took me so low.
We all have demons in hiding until they're exposed.

So, with that, I let go of the pain.
I remember your name not with hate,

but remain in peace

with the past
and what we had.

Breaking Cycles

I don't need validation when the love ain't real,
when it's not a soul connection,
when it's a karmic deal.

You got fear in your mind, but I got love in my heart.
You can't keep the promises you make,
can't finish what you start.

I caught you in a lie, time after time,
until I had enough and finally said ... goodbye.

◆━━━━━━

Mending Love

"Never will I fall so deeply in love again,"
I kept telling myself.

I refused to take part in this wicked game,
for a broken heart doesn't leave you the same.

Yours was a love I never felt before—
a gentle knock
I opened the door, letting you into the deepest parts of me.

Like a house of mirrors, all you could see
was yourself in your entirety.

Like a wave in the sea, you came and went.
Leaving trails of your essence—it was hard to lose the scent.

The deeper part of me knows you and I were meant to be.
Lovers from a past life, a love from another galaxy.

Red String of Fate

A love like yours
isn't easy to find.

Yet it came to me
at an unexpected time.

When I stopped looking,
that's when you found me.

Oceans apart, love brought us together.

Bound by the red string,
we are two souls meant to be.

———————

Heartbreak Endures

Your love for me faded
as the seasons changed.

My love for you endures
even in the company of your absence.

You promised me I'll find
someone else to hold and love.

Little do you know, the gods have written
your name across the surface of my heart.

Abandoned Potential

Am I wrong for holding on
to the thought of
what we could be?
You left me no choice but to move on.

Now I'm left with my anxiety.

Love Fades, Yet Its Memory Lingers

Time has elapsed,
and with time, I detached.

A new lover has made their way,
and I don't know if they'll stay.

But every love song that plays
still reminds me of you.

Human Love

My fragile heart can't take the abuse of lovers
who don't know what to do
when someone loves them for the first time.

The past hijacks their mind,
and the fear creeps in—that's when they resign.

I want a love that stays,
a love that won't evade me
in either my joy or misery.

I want that special someone who will be
my ride-or-die for eternity.

Is this a fantasy that will never come to be?

Help me, God,
find true love,
change the tide of my destiny!

The Dark Pit of Self

A Sensitive Soul Grows Weary

I descend into darkness, where I sit with my shadows.
I reflect on and question all that I know.
It's just God and I in this season of isolation.
It is here where I move through the trials and tribulations.

Spiritual Warfare

It appears as if there is no way out.
I'm drowning in the darkness; the voices are getting loud.

It's a crime to have a mind that can turn against you.
There's nowhere to turn to.

They say the path is within you.

Head above water, I barely catch a breath.
My eyes seek the sky—has my time come yet?

Now, I begin to see clearly all that stands before me.

Nothing feels the same.

Am I going insane?

Everything seems fake.

The Truth brings pain to a soul carrying something real,
and others don't see it the same way.

I'm fighting demons; I plead to the angels
to come to my rescue and protect me from every angle.

Self-Protection

It's hard to trust anyone.
I question their intentions.

I can't let them in.

Experience has shown me
there's no good reason to let them.

I keep my energy secure,
for I can never be sure
they mean what they say.

Loyalty is hard to come by.
It's easy to say goodbye
when the going gets tough.

They'll say: that's life, suck it up.

That's why I move with a fence around my presence.
Cloaked in incense, my spiritual sense is my protection.

◆━━━━━━

A Longing for Depth

Loneliness consumes me.
Sadness builds its home within.

It feels like no one hears me,

even when I'm screaming,

even when my heart is bleeding

from the knives in my back
put in by people from my past.

Where the real ones at?

Hazy Thoughts

I can't seem to see past my own anxiety.

Locked in the den, I try to befriend
the lions in my mind.

I try to act like it's fine.

But it's not.
It's a lot to live with these roaring thoughts,
but to live with them has taught me they're nothing but
a lie.

As fleeting as clouds that glide through the sky.

With awareness, I'm assured I'm all right.

I'm all right.

The Sea Speaks

I look out to the sea. "Can you hear me?" I say.
"Do you feel this grief I bury inside me day by day?"

"My child," Mother Ocean replies, "you are not alone.
You must experience each wave, its every high and low,
to see how much you can grow."

Phoenix

From dust we rise,
and to dust we shall return.

This life is but a game,
a game you have chosen to play.

And play you must.

Break Free

I want to fly away to the sky.
I'll reach new heights.
I'm gone,
night and day.

When I'm in my own world,
I'm fine.
I'm okay.
Nothing's standing in my way.

Running With the Wolves

I run with the wolves and rise with the waves.
A spirit untamed, I am liberated in the best ways.

For nature is my compass, and to Her I turn.
In my glory and misery, from Her I learn.

"Stay close to me," She gently whispers.
"Remember who you are.
You and I are one and the same;
you need not seek me from afar."

Interconnected

When you feel lonely,
look up at the night sky.

In the glow of the moon and the sparkle of the star,
you will find me.

An Old Friend

A wave of nostalgia washes over me
as I lift my head to gaze at the night sky.
A smile naturally forms on my face; my body is showered
with a profound sense of ease and peace.

The stars seem to wink back at me with every sparkle,
like an old friend.
The moon's warm glow touches the deepest parts of me.

I look with intention, to feel the wisdom of the cosmos—
the place from which I come
and to which I shall one day

return.

I bask in the moving cosmic image before me,
and I know, deep within, I am never alone here.

Paradox

What a blessing and curse it is to be deeply sensitive—
to feel the world, its embrace and grip, so intensely.

I can be shattered by the faintest pain
and uplifted to the heavens by the smallest joy.

In my sensitivity, I exist in the extremes,
working tirelessly to find the middle, where relief awaits me.

Strength in Sensitivity

My sensitivity is a badge I proudly wear.
I carry the history of my ancestors—a calling noble and fair.

In my conscious awareness of all that is,
I heal my lineage with a sweet, gentle kiss.

From the Ashes

A New Dawn

I gave to the world, and the world left me empty.
I brought the warmth, but the cold didn't spare me.

Is the world at fault for bringing me to my knees?

Or did it open my eyes and teach me how to finally see?

In our darkest moments, we can't help but point the finger
when we carry all the hurt as it sits and lingers.

There is purpose in pain, even if you're not to blame.
If you want to see a difference, you need to make the change.

Rise above.
Don't ever stay down.

Hold your ground and your crown.
Let your aura be loud.

You're magic,
you're stardust,
you're Divine in human form.

Don't fear the rainy days.
Remember: you're the storm.

Calm After the Storm

What peculiar creatures humans are!

Lost in the noise of their minds,
from the silent pull of Spirit, they traverse far.

They made the world the source of all their glory.
They relinquish their power to the same old story.

I cannot pass judgment, for I was the same.
Blinded by ignorance, I tried to fit in and play the game.

But I lived, and I learned.

I came out the other side.
I woke up to the truth and let go of the lie.

For what good will it do if I lost my own soul
to fit in a world that lacks love for all?

True power, real love, rests within.

No, it's not a sin to connect with your intuition.

Let your heart be the compass; let Spirit take the lead.
Grow a New Earth, and let love be the seed.

Beyond the Surface

I carry my heart like a pot of gold.
Connected to Spirit, it can never be sold.

Our society sees the body as same.

But what remains when our bodies go to the grave?

The memory of you is reflected
in Soul,
in the energy you bring,
in the love you show,

and in the seeds you sow

in another's heart.

Divine Love

In a world that confuses lust with love, I implore you,
don't follow the trend; the lesson will be rough.

You're more than a body; you're more than the surface.
True beauty is intrinsic; it's felt and amorphous.

Your spirit is the light that makes the way.
With compassion in your heart, you can work to save
yourself

and then those who are still asleep.

It's time to take the lead, my darling black sheep!

Consciousness Unity

I see the world in colors;
they see it in black and white.

To keep it simple, they teach us
everyone must pick a side.

I don't care who you are.
I don't care where you're from.

We're all one Consciousness.
I care what's in your heart.

Recalibration

To be awake
when everyone's asleep
will make you think

you're slowly sinking into insanity
where it's fine to be
yourself
everything, nothing and the in-between.

There's a fine line between
losing your mind and seeing the light.

But I don't mind:

I'll never lose sight of the Truth.

Yes, it's true.
When you wake up, the world will seem new.

You'll start to see vividly
all is not what it seems.

Your old world will shake, a sudden earthquake.
Your old world will break, but it's for your own sake.

Creative Sovereignty

Your experience of life is the story you tell yourself about it.
It can be good or bad, positive or bleak.
One thing's for sure: You'll find what you seek.

———————

Beyond the Veil

My soul has had its dark nights;
I endured the pain for it to open my eyes.

The Truth has set me free
from the illusion I need to be
anything other than myself.

The Truth has taught me
there's more to this space and time reality.

Don't be deceived by what you see.

The Promised Land

I lived, and I learned.
I loved, and I lost.

I've had to bear my cross.
At every cost, I healed

to reach the Promised Land.

Love Transforms

Love is a foreign concept to the world of humans.
Vulnerability seems daunting—it's left people in ruins.

Love isn't romance.

It's a state of being—
a gentle dance
between acceptance and respect.

It's more than just chemistry and sex.

It's an attitude, an approach to life.

Give more of it, not less.

It has the power to drive change.
It's the only thing that keeps us sane.

Move with love: you've got nothing to lose
but everything to gain.

Master or Be Mastered

The ego turns to pride when you feed it.
Turn back, it's a trap—you'll get defeated.

You see, the ego can't be satisfied.
Like a child, it'll start to cry.

It wants what it wants;
it wants to take the apple of its eye.

The ego attaches itself to that which is temporary.
In the material world, it finds its sanctuary.

Nothing lasts forever.
This world is but a dream.

Eternal is the Spirit.
This Truth will set you free.

Stand Alone

I've learned to make my own way.
I don't fear being alone.

If you leave, it's your mistake;
I won't convince you to stay.

Take your leave, then,
if you so desire.

I'll throw the memories of you into the fire.

A Tower Moment

The Truth will set you free, but at first, it's a bitch.
A bitter pill to swallow. A bitter pill you can't spit.

But once it dissolves, it becomes sweet like honey.
Food for the soul, your world becomes sunny.

If you choose to—that's the key here.

The choice is yours between love and fear.

It can make you or break you.
To the darkest places, it can take you.

But just know

God will never forsake you.

A good day is coming.

A new dawn won't escape you.

Love Is a State of Being

I've been looking for love in all the wrong places.
It's been the same old love with different faces.

I didn't know what it meant to love myself
until I got jaded with the disrespect.
I couldn't fake it.

Little did I know, I was the love of my life.

It took a while to get there;
the path wasn't always nice.

I'm grateful for all the lessons learned.

The pain became the portal.

I set my old ways on fire and watched that shit burn.

◆━━━━━

Beyond the Tears, A Rainbow Awaits

I forget the number of times I cried myself to sleep,
my eyes burning red with passionate release.

Is life supposed to always feel this way?
I was under the impression
I'd be subject to a life of subtle depression.

Because of the way I feel things so deeply,
I always thought there was something wrong with me.

But there's nothing wrong with feeling something
in a world where people keep on running
from feeling anything at all.

I know there's purpose in not being the same.
Through my sensitivity, I bring sunshine to the rain.

Through my sensitivity, I understand other people's pain.

Through my sensitivity, I teach people
there's nothing to be ashamed of

in

feeling something.

Look No Further Than Yourself

I enjoy things with soul,
for it is in depth you'll find gold.

Your body is the shell,
your Spirit the pearl.

And that's where you'll find
all you're looking for.

Cosmic DNA

Life is not about looks, wealth or fame.
To the Higher Self, that's lame.

It's who you are beneath all that.
Recognize we are all the same.

We come from Love and are made up of stardust.

One with the Universe, the answers lie within.

Meditate and closely listen to your intuition.
The depths of your being guide your soul's mission.

Creation Is One

The night must always follow the day.
The cycles of nature are always the same.

Even in our lives, it applies.
The sun doesn't always shine;
the sky sometimes cries.

Let these patterns in nature remind us
of the transient ways of this life.

Embrace the Paradox

Enjoy the good days,
have courage in the bad.

Stand strong in faith,
and know this too shall pass.

Those in the Shadows

Love takes work; it's not always perfect.
But in the end, the work is always worth it.

Good things take time; I guess that's why
many people leave when they get tired.

In the modern world, we think we have many options—
many lovers to choose from in a world of abundance.

But, then

what does love mean when everyone can see
the most special parts of you that you give so freely?

Please believe not everyone is meant to be
for you or close to you: protect your energy.

Sometimes it takes life to open your eyes
to see that some people are a devil in disguise.

Awakening

With tears in my eyes, I look up to the sky.
The sun meets my face in a gentle embrace.

My thoughts dissipate as I take a deep breath.
I take in the calm and exhale the distress.

In this moment with God, I realize who I am.

I'm Spirit in the flesh, nothing more than "I Am."

I lift my hands in praise, thanking the Father for His ways
for His love and strength, which carry me through my days.

Returning Home

I turned my eyes away from God.

I moved away from what I knew.
I tried to find my place in the world
when I didn't have a clue.

I was stupid, I was young, I was curious.
I sought out adventure; back then, life was less serious.

They say ignorance is bliss,
but ignorance became a bitch
when I followed the crowd and my sense of self drowned.

I wasn't made to fit in. I knew this from early on.

But it didn't take long for me to learn and catch on:

This world is an illusion, with many in delusion
about who they are and what they want.
Conditioning creates the confusion.

The path less traveled is one of the hardest to take.
But this life chose me; it's not something I can escape.

And I wouldn't want to.

It's shaped me into who I am today.

It taught me how to have faith when I couldn't find a way.

It brought me back to the Source of All
and allowed me to
lead with soul.

Wisdom Awaits on the Other Side

I embarked on the Fool's Journey, and a fool I've been,
thinking I'd make it unscathed in this world of sin.

But then, I realized what a blessing it is
to take off my rose-colored glasses
and see the world for what it is.

I took a leap of faith and went down the rabbit hole.
I dug a little deep and was met by a dark night of the soul.

It took some time
to find the light,
the spark within
that once burned bright.

but this time,
I'm moving differently.

God is the ground beneath my feet;
He guides my steps with gentle ease.

I'm free from the things that held me back.

It's out with the old and in with the new.

When the calling is higher, there's no room
for anything that doesn't serve the Highest Good.

Still Human

I haven't reached the peak of the mountain.

No human can.
The climb never ends.

The top isn't important
because it doesn't exist.

The only thing that matters is the view—
so, enjoy it.

There's a lesson with every milestone.
Yes, you'll stumble and fall,

Yet

You'll grow into the person you were meant to be.
You'll break from your shell and set your soul free.

Please believe, your pain is not in vain.
Let it make you, not break you,
by embracing the inner change.

Every experience is leading you back home to your soul.
So, be gentle with yourself.

You're still human after all.

ABOUT THE AUTHOR

Emma Stefania is a writer based in Brooklyn, New York. While devoted to the written word, she enjoys exploring various art forms, including photography and videography, as means of creative expression and visual storytelling.

In 2019, Emma began her spiritual journey after being Divinely led toward a spiritual awakening. Her experiences have deepened her interests in spirituality, mysticism, philosophy and religion, compelling her to convey the esoteric wisdom she has gained—and continues to receive and channel—in her writings.

She holds a Master of Science in Journalism from Columbia University.

You can follow her on Instagram @thenoblewriter and @beyondthemomentart.